Prairie Visions:

The Life and Times of

SOLOMON BUTCHER

PAM CONRAD

SCHOLASTIC INC.
New York Toronto London Auckland Sydney

Very particular thanks to—

The Society of Children's Book Writers

for yet another Works in Progress Grant,

the very knowledgeable John Carter in Lincoln,

the Holoun Retreat Center,

the dedicated teacher and learner Jean Birth,

and Jo Hansen, my Nebraska soddy sister

ISBN 0-590-46116-8

12 11 10 9 8 7 6 5 4 3 2   2 3 4 5 6 7/9

Printed in the U.S.A.   08

First Scholastic printing, September 1992

Prairie Visions

dedicated to my father,

who, when I was very young,

showed me how pictures could develop

—magically—

in the chemicals, in the dark

This mother insisted Butcher photograph only the things she was proud of. The soddy stands behind the camera, unphotographed.

Contents

Prairie Visions

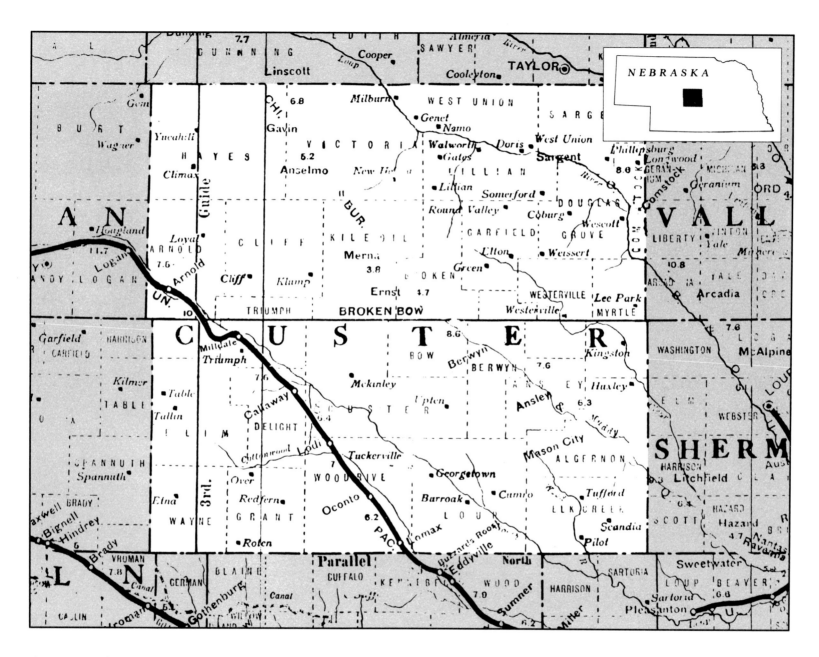

A 1915 map of Custer County; the inset shows the county within Nebraska.

Introduction

I remember the day I first discovered Solomon Butcher. I was doing research for my novel *Prairie Songs* in the archives at the Nebraska State Historical Society in Lincoln, and the minute I saw all the pictures he had taken of Nebraska pioneers, I knew I wanted him to take a picture of the pioneer family in my book as well. So using what little information I had, I "made him up." Studying a couple of old photographs of him, I made up how he might have talked, what he would have looked like, and that he probably would have smelled like photographic chemicals. And then without effort, Solomon Butcher came to life. He rode his wagon over the hill into my story, eager to photograph the Downing family along with the frail and troubled Emmeline Berryman.

I loved Solomon Butcher, just as I loved Louisa and Lester and all the other characters that had come to me during the writing of *Prairie Songs*.

Then one day, after my novel had been published, I was speaking (as a historical novelist) to a group of teachers in Grand Island, Nebraska. After the talk when I was signing books, a woman came over to me and asked me to sign two copies of *Prairie Songs*, one for herself and one for her neighbor—Solomon Butcher's daughter. A shiver ran through me. It was as though there had been a tug on my skirt and, turning around, I'd found Lester there.

Hadn't I made Solomon Butcher up? Wasn't he a figment of my imagination? No. He'd been a real man, and suddenly I wanted to know all there was to know about him. So I returned once again to the archives in Lincoln and peered more deeply this time into his history, reaching back with both hands to this most unusual man.

What I like most about Solomon Butcher is that he was not satisfied with being merely a portraitist. Although he began his career taking formal portraits, his vision expanded, and soon he needed to include more than simply faces to capture the true life and nature of his subjects. It was then that he stood back and shot a broad, bold picture—people set in the drama of their everyday lives. He'd photograph a family before their homestead with their horses to the side and a windmill behind them; he took a picture of a woman and her family around a piano that had been brought outdoors, with the cattle as background; and he

This is how I pictured J.T. and Clara Downing in Prairie Songs.

showed a family standing and sitting in a line, with slices of watermelon in their hands and their mysterious eyes squinting into the sun. Of all the photographers of his day, there was no one quite like Solomon Butcher. His vision is unmistakable.

I have tried to follow suit. This is not a literary portrait of Solomon Butcher, with his face in sharp focus. Instead I have tried to step back and capture this man in his life, surrounded by his family, his stories, and his dreams. And if—as some believe his subjects were—he'd been asked to haul out his prize possession for this portrait, I believe he would have brought out these photographs and these tales.

I can feel the watermelon juice running through my fingers.

Someone's little sister fell asleep and missed this picture taking. She would be nearly 100 years old today.

MY FIRST HOUSE IN NEB. 1880 BUILT FROM "NEB. BRICK"

Of course we know what "Nebraska brick" was—blocks of sod.

The Reluctant Pioneer

Solomon Butcher was a man of big ideas, a man with a vision. Born in the century before ours, in 1856, in a small town in what is now West Virginia, he never stayed very long in one spot, or stuck very long at anything he tried to do. After he graduated from high school in 1874, he became an apprentice to a tintypist and learned the new art and science of photography, but he did not immediately become a photographer. He went on to spend one term in a military school in Illinois before he hit the road for four years as a traveling salesman.

Who knows how long he would have wandered around aimlessly, but in 1880 his father, Thomas Jefferson Butcher, was swept away by pioneer fever and announced that he, his wife, and the rest of the family were going to claim some homesteads in Custer County, Nebraska.

This appealed to Solomon Butcher, and being a man of adventure, when his father, brother George, and brother-in-law J. R. Wabel set out in covered wagons for the promised land of Nebraska, Solomon was with them. For seven hundred miles they plodded along from sunup till sundown, averaging a hundred miles a week. Now our man of adventure had never slept out under the stars before, or lived under less than comfortable conditions, so it wasn't long before he was sick, and his father—seeing as how Solomon wasn't good for anything else—appointed him to the job of cook.

When the Butcher men finally arrived in Custer County, they each staked a claim and had to build houses to prove their claims. Houses in Nebraska were built of sod bricks and the work was hard. Even though they hadn't completed their soddies and had run out of food (they were eating food they had brought for the animals), Thomas Jefferson Butcher felt confident enough to return home to Illinois and get his wife and youngest son, Abner.

Solomon went back East with his father, but didn't return to Nebraska. He stayed on in Illinois for almost six months, probably never wanting to return to Nebraska at all, but at the last minute, with only three days left to build a house on his own claim, he sped back to Nebraska and built it. Then after only two weeks of hard work, with four and a half long years stretching ahead of him as the Homestead Act required, he changed his mind once again. He gave his land back to the government and left Nebraska.

From there he went to Minneapolis to attend medical school. His new scheme was to become a doctor. That must have been hard work, too, because Solomon lasted only a year. But it wasn't a total loss. At the hospital he met a lovely nurse—Lillie Barber Hamilton—whom he married, and with ideas of more adventure in his mind, which now included someone to help with the work and the cooking, Solomon Butcher took his wife to Custer County and they moved in with his father. He bought a piece of land and on it—still scheming—he built the first photographic gallery in Custer County. Here farmers and their families could have their portraits taken to send home to relatives to show how prosperous they had become.

This gallery was far from the ideal artist's studio. It was made of adobe, or mud, the walls and floors were rough and dirty, and to create as much light as possible there were windows and skylights in the roof covered with cotton fabric. Despite its roughness, on a bright Nebraska afternoon the studio must have glowed inside.

Solomon Butcher fashioned a portrait setting for his customers where they could sit and hold very still before his camera. As a backdrop he made do with an old canvas wagon cover that the rats had gotten hold of.

Solomon Butcher, pioneer

photographer

This is Tom Smith who was a boxer, a tough man, and editor of the West Union Gazette. *Butcher's wife, Lillie Barber Hamilton*

Lillie tried to patch it, but the poor patches showed in the picture, until Solomon had a good idea. He hung bedsprings from the ceiling and attached the wagon cover to them, and when it was time to take a picture, the cloth was sent dancing on its springs and the patches became barely visible blurs to the camera's eye.

But this life of a portrait photographer was very difficult and business was unpredictable. If the local farmers had a good year with crops and prices, they could afford to have their pictures taken. But if it was a bad year, a photograph seemed like a silly luxury. And who would want to send pictures home to show how tired and old they were becoming?

In a more practical attempt to make a living, Solomon Butcher opened a post office in 1882, but the remaining records show he made only sixty eight cents in three months.

When Solomon and Lillie's son Lynn was born in 1883, they moved out of his father's soddy and into this muddy, bright photo gallery. It wasn't too bad, except when it rained and the roof leaked. Then they would have to return to his father's. Solomon complained that he certainly couldn't repair the roof when it was raining, and when the sun was shining, well, then the roof didn't *need* repairing. He was often accused of being afraid of work, as you can imagine, but he claimed he wasn't afraid of work at all. "On the contrary," he had said, "I could lie down and go to sleep along side of it at any time."

A year later a daughter, Madge, was born. Struggling to make a living in any odd fashion that he could, Solomon took a job as a schoolteacher, made frames, farmed for his father, and tried to keep the gallery going through hard times and rainy weeks.

The families in the area got together and built this sod schoolhouse. Children of all ages learned together.

In Prairie Songs *Louisa said she saw Butcher coming over the hill in his wagon and he looked like "a circus performer or a carnival act."*

His Vision

One day in 1886, when Solomon Butcher was at the end of his rope and none of his schemes had made him rich, he had a vision—a bright idea. He decided to create a photographic history of Custer County, Nebraska, a kind of documentary of prairie life as it was happening. His family thought he was crazy. After all, they thought, Custer County was so new it didn't even *have* a history yet, but Solomon Butcher knew history was in the making. Undaunted, he went to town and in two weeks managed to sign up seventy-five families to be photographed. His father was impressed and agreed to give him a wagon and the supplies he would need. Solomon Butcher was on the road again.

He traveled for hours and hours over difficult rut roads, but this time didn't tire. He accepted food, lodging, and the stabling of his horses for copies of his photographs. He supported himself with donations, sales of photographs, and subscriptions—promises for this history book that would one day—he was sure—be published.

Solomon Butcher would ride up to a farm in his wagon and tell about his dream. Some historians believe he told the farmers to bring out their favorite possessions to be photographed too, which accounts for the musical instruments and framed portraits and lace doilies. Yet other historians say people left those things outside the soddy anyway, seeing as how the soddies were so crowded and the Nebraska days were so dry. Whichever it was, before they knew it, the family who lived there would stand in front of their soddy for Solomon Butcher, facing the south and the sun, grim-looking and squinting, or turning their heads to the side and away from the glare. It obviously didn't occur to the majority of the pioneers to ham it up for the camera, or even to smile.

This is one of Butcher's accounts of the actual picture-taking process:

We drove up to a settler's house to take a picture of it, with the family group in front. Before we could get the camera focused, one of the children, a lad of seven or eight years, made a break for the tall grass that was growing about three feet high in the vicinity, and hid. The balance of the family hunted for him about a quarter of an hour while we stood patiently awaiting the round-up in the boiling sun. They were unsuccessful in their search, and returned to have the group taken without him. Just as we were about ready to make the exposure, away went another of the

Can you see the little boy's arm in a sling? Despite hardships this mother smiled.

I can imagine one of these boys making a break for the tall grasses!

boys, which resulted in another hunt and another failure. Then the old man got mad and said: "Take what you've got." I secured six of the children and the two old people. Two of them got away for sure, and how many more I did not stop to figure out, but left that for the parents when they counted noses.

Butcher's adventures didn't take place only during the taking of pictures. He also did some rather unorthodox retouching back at the studio during his career—such as adding trees and flying ducks. He even painted a descending swarm of locusts around a photograph of one Ephram Swain Finch—the very man who would eventually play an important role in the publication of Butcher's book.

And once he accidentally damaged a negative so that it looked like there was a big hole in the roof of one particular family's soddy. Not wanting to travel back sixty miles and take another picture, he retouched the photo by painting what he thought looked like a turkey covering the hole.

The story goes that when Butcher delivered the photograph, the homesteader stared at the photo and said, "What is that?"

Butcher answered, "Why, it looks like a turkey to me."

"Couldn't be a turkey," the homesteader said. "The turkeys weren't around that day. Besides . . . we don't have any white ones."

The homesteader's wife drew near and looked at the photo too. "Yes,

Theodore," she said, "don't you remember me telling you to drive the turkeys away?"

Strangely enough that settled it, and without further argument that farmer paid for the portrait of his family. Looking at the photo today, it's hard to believe the farmer could have accepted that it was really a turkey. This probably illustrates not so much the naïveté and unsophisticated eye of a nineteenth-century farmer, but rather the ability of the farmer's wife to smooth a quarrel.

In the next seven years Solomon Butcher took more than fifteen hundred photographs. He also collected stories, biographies, and anecdotes from the people of the county, the pioneers he wanted to preserve for all time. He was a "pioneer who photographed pioneers."

On the following pages are a few of the stories and some of the pictures he gathered up during those times. "These are the facts," he said, "as I got them from one who was there."

Does that "turkey" fool you?

Aunt Sarah here laughed at Uncle Swain when he threw himself into a snowbank to die.

Accounts

Snowbank Suicide

Solomon Butcher heard this story about the old couple named Uncle Swain and Aunt Sarah who were stuck in their soddy for days on end one winter, with the snow piled high around them. (The uncle is the same Ephram Swain Finch who later became very important to Butcher's vision.) Their two young nephews, Johnny and Bob, were staying with them, and nerves were raw, tempers short. On one particularly tense morning Aunt Sarah was giving Uncle Swain a piece of her mind while the boys sat quietly by. Suddenly Uncle Swain yelled at her:

"If you don't shut right up, I'll go out and freeze myself to death in the snowbank."

The boys stared wide-eyed. They'd never heard such talk. But Aunt Sarah kept right on laying down the law as she saw it. So with his teeth clenched and his eyes staring straight ahead, Uncle Swain took down his overcoat and put it on, buttoning it up to his chin. His nephews thought he'd gone crazy for sure. They watched openmouthed as he marched out of the soddy. They ran to the woodshed to watch him through a chink in the wood. From there they saw him walk a ways from the house and lie down in a snowbank.

They waited, and after a few minutes the freezing man raised himself up on one elbow and looked back at the soddy. He must have seen his nephews peering out at him from the woodshed, for he signaled them to come to him.

"Go get me my buffalo robe, Johnny," he ordered.

Johnny ran back to the soddy and got it. They stared at him as he wrapped it carefully around his body and once again lay down to freeze, now in comfort.

He stayed there a long time, and the boys went back to the soddy and watched through the deep window. Finally after a while he motioned to them again. The boys ran out and stared down at him.

"Say, boys," he whispered, "is the old gal a-cryin'?"

"Naw," Bob answered. "She's laughin'."

"That settles it," Uncle Swain shouted, standing up and shaking out his buffalo robe. "Then I *won't* freeze." And he went back in the soddy.

When Coffee Was Coffee

An old settler who remembered the 1830s told Solomon this story. Early pioneers loved their coffee, and the greatest find in the world, something akin to buried treasure, would be the discovery of a sugar barrel full of coffee at an old abandoned campsite. But the coffee was sometimes disappointing if not downright disgusting.

Solomon heard the story about some ranchhands who were gathered around the coffeepot one morning. They had each had three or four cups when they noticed something white on the bottom of the pot.

These look like men who loved their coffee strong and black without anything added.

"Where'd you get that egg in the bottom of the coffeepot, Jim?" they asked the cook.

"There's no egg," Jim grumbled.

"But I can see an egg," the ranchhand said.

They all followed Jim out into the yard, where he took the coffeepot and dumped it on the grass. No one wanted any more coffee after that, and they were all sorry they had drunk as much as they had. For there in the grass, covered with coffee grounds, was the body of a dead frog swollen to three times its usual size. The poor senseless frog had probably fallen off the wall into the pot during the night.

Grasshopper Storm

Then there were the terrible accounts of grasshopper plagues. In the spring of 1876 the farmers were watching their ears of corn swell and become ready for harvesting, when suddenly what looked like a prairie fire smudged the northwest horizon. But it couldn't have been a prairie fire. The grass was too green and moist. The farmers watched in wonder as it grew closer and grew noisier, with crackings and snappings and then a roar as millions of grasshoppers surrounded them. The cornstalks were stripped clean. A fence post the size of a man's arm, soon covered

Can you tell Butcher drew these locusts around Uncle Swain?

with grasshoppers, became as thick as a log. No amount of threshing or stomping or smoking could stop them. They ate and ate until they were full. When it was over, the farms looked like a fire had indeed just swept through.

Restless Night

A man named Jess Gandy told Solomon Butcher about a hunting trip where he and his companion had shot several deer and were well pleased with the prize they were bringing home to be skinned and quartered and prepared for food and hides. On the way home it began to rain, and they decided to spend the night in an old abandoned soddy. Weary and exhausted, they tossed their bedding onto a pile of leaves and weeds that had blown into the corner and then lay down and immediately fell asleep.

After a while Jess woke up thinking he felt something moving beneath his bed of weeds. But his friend was sound asleep and snoring, so he thought maybe it was his imagination. He tried to go back to sleep, but suddenly the ground beneath them was heaving and tossing and tumbling. They both were wide awake now, and suddenly the tossing stopped, and they could see a family of small animals parade out the

Andy Howland borrowed money on his claim and disappeared. His brother believed he was murdered and offered a reward for any trace of him.

door. In the darkness it was hard to see clearly, but they could tell that these were small creatures, furry and black, and that they had white stripes down their backs! Jess and his friend had fallen asleep atop a family of skunks.

Toting Snow

Some homesteaders were very bright. And maybe not too impressed by book learning. They liked to hear a good story about someone who was supposedly intelligent but without much common sense. For instance, they loved the story of Judge Kilgore, who, with all his education and knowledge, carried water home two miles every day for weeks through two feet of snow. Imagine the smile on the homesteader's face who finally asked the judge why didn't he melt the snow right outside his door for water?

Adventure of One J. D. Strong

J. D. Strong wrote to Solomon Butcher about what it was like to travel across the prairie in those early days. He'd had many adventures. On one trip it was growing very dark while he was trying to follow a dim trail. He needed a place to stay, and pioneer families in Nebraska were usually grateful for a little company and glad to put out an extra dish for dinner and a cot for a passing stranger.

Soon J. D. came upon what he was pretty sure was a fence post, and thinking he'd come to a farmer's fence, he touched it and felt for wires. But it wasn't a post at all. It was warm and soon he realized it was a stovepipe and that he was standing on the roof of someone's dugout— a home dug into a bank with dirt walls, dirt floor, and dirt ceiling. His team was right behind him and in danger of crashing right through the roof onto the sleepers below. Slowly he backed the team up away from the dugout, and went back to look for the door. He couldn't tell where the bank ended and the dugout began, and suddenly he lost his footing in the darkness, went tumbling down the bank through a window, and landed on the cooking utensils, making enough noise to stampede a bunch of plow horses. There were wild shouts of: "Who's there?" "Get out!" "Scat!" "Get a light!" "Get the gun!"

Pulling himself up out of the jumble of milk crocks, tinware, kettles, and frying pans, J. D. Strong made a hasty retreat back out the window, and as quickly as he could, he found his way around to the door. In the midst of the commotion inside, he knocked as a civilized man should,

Imagine coming upon a soddy like this in the dark, just as J. D. Strong did.

and once a light was lit and the damage assessed, the McEndeffer family gave J. D. Strong some food and a place to spend the night, as he had hoped they would.

J. D. Strong continued his journey the next day, and had the dubious privilege of spending the next night in what might be loosely termed the first hotel in Broken Bow, a small soddy owned by C. D. Pelham who could easily stow away thirteen men in one small room, with only six blankets. It was said he used to remove the blankets from the ones who were sleeping to give to the new arrivals, and if it was cold and the first sleeper awoke, the next guest would soon fall asleep and C. D. Pelham would restore the blanket to the original owner. By shifting and switching like this through the night, he could keep all his guests as warm as pie on the coldest night, even though every one of them would be uncovered most of the time.

The night that J. D. Strong spent at C. D. Pelham's there weren't too many guests, and he settled himself down comfortably under his own warm blanket. But it wasn't long before he felt a crawling, hopping, biting sensation. He tossed and turned and itched and scratched, trying desperately to sleep, until he finally realized that C. D. Pelham's hotel was full of fleas, and he would never get any sleep. Gathering up his bedding, he went out to sleep under the stars, but the fleas were in his blankets now, too. Abandoning his blankets and shaking out his clothes, he finally settled down on the top of a woodpile and left his bedclothes for the fleas.

J. D. Strong reminded Solomon Butcher that no history of Custer County could be complete without including a story about the fleas, for they respected no one—not man, woman, or child, not soddy or church—and because of that, it was never impolite in Custer County to scratch any particular part of your body that happened to be itching.

On one other of J. D. Strong's journeys, in the heart of the winter when it was extremely cold, he was staying on with a pioneer family in

I can see where this family hid when a tornado threatened.

their small soddy. He arose early and started the fire for the family and put a loaf of bread he had brought with him into the oven to thaw. He was having his coffee when one of the ladies in the family came and sat on the opposite side of the stove. After a while he reached for his bread to eat it, and discovered that she had her feet on his loaf! She had thought it was a brick. J. D. later said he wouldn't have minded if it had been a graceful foot, but it was a short, fat foot, with chubby toes. Life was hard on the prairie.

Outlaw for Breakfast

No one ever likes to be treated poorly after extending kindness and hospitality to a stranger. The Nebraska homesteader was no different, only it was well worth it and made a great tale to tell when the stranger was a celebrity of sorts.

Solomon Butcher heard this tale of how early one morning Mr. Downey and his wife were just stirring from sleep in their little soddy nestled in the hills. Mr. Downey was getting his overalls on, and Mrs. Downey was building a small fire to make some breakfast, when they noticed a stranger approaching the house on foot. He was refined-looking, fashionably dressed in a Prince Albert coat. He was stout and dark, with a pair of glittering dark eyes.

"Can you give me some breakfast and show me the way to the South Loop?" the stranger asked.

"I think we can," answered Mrs. Downey, "if you can put up with the kind of grub we poor folks are living on."

Mr. Downey added, "That road yonder is called Plum Creek Road, and it will take you straight to the South Loop in about fifty miles. But that's a long way. Why are you on foot?"

"I'm expecting to meet up with some friends," explained the horseless stranger. "They will probably overtake me soon."

Silently they shared a meager breakfast together, and when they were done the stranger asked if he could rest awhile before continuing on. Mr. Downey said that was fine with him, but he had work to do, and would be on his way out to the fields.

Mr. Downey was gone a short while when the stranger took down a rifle from the wall and a belt full of loaded shells. To Mrs. Downey's astonishment he put the belt around his own waist, tucked the rifle under his arm, and started out the door.

"Wait! What are you doin', sir?" Mrs. Downey cried. "Drop that gun or I'll call my husband, who's not far off."

"Go ahead and call him," said the stranger, "but I need this gun in my business and I intend to take it. Good day." And he started off for the main road.

"John! John!" shouted Mrs. Downey, and she rang the warning bell on top of the soddy.

Mr. Downey came running with his pitchfork in hand, and when his wife told him what had happened, he went running down the road after the stranger, demanding the return of his property. But a pitchfork and a rifle are not equal contestants.

The bell on this roof could call everyone home, as the one in Prairie Songs *did.*

"Go on about your business, farmer, and you won't have any trouble. And you won't have your head blown off either."

And at that the stranger adjusted the farmer's ammunition belt on his own waist, turned his back, and walked on to Plum Creek Road.

Word came soon after that a stranger was seen some thirty-five miles north, leaning on his rifle and staring northwest. He was refined-looking, fashionably dressed in a Prince Albert coat. He was stout and dark, with a pair of glittering dark eyes. And it was said he was none other than the notorious Jack Nolan, outlaw and gambler. Mr. Downey loved to tell how Nolan had just murdered a man down in Mexico and had broken out of jail at Plum Creek right before he'd been their guest.

Homesteaders could never be sure what interesting new event would be heading up the road at them early in the morning.

The Jack Nolan Escape

Of course when Mr. Downey would tell that story about Jack Nolan coming for breakfast to whomever would listen, there would always be those who could add to it.

"But did you hear how Jack Nolan escaped from the Plum Creek jail just before that?" they'd ask.

It seems Jack Nolan was arrested and was awaiting trial in the small local jail. And there was a young boy who worked there named Gatch Hughey. It was Gatch's job to bring the prisoners their meals. He must have been pretty intimidated to have the notorious Jack Nolan there, for Nolan was known to be the most wild and daring of all outlaws in central Nebraska.

One evening, with the sun going down in the west and a hot wind howling across the prairie, Jack Nolan called to the boy. "Hey, Gatch, can't you give us a song?"

Gatch, who they said would rather sing than work any day, began belting out a song that lasted a long time. He sang verse after verse, chorus after chorus all by heart, and when he was finally done he sat there grinning and expecting to hear some kind of applause from the cell where Jack Nolan was locked.

Not a sound. He got up and looked into the cell, only to discover it was empty. The bars had been sawed away and the outlaw was nowhere to be seen.

Of course when a homesteader told this story to Solomon Butcher for his book, there was some speculation. What do you think? they wondered. Was Gatch telling the truth? Or was he in cahoots with the outlaw? I wonder.

This farmer must have done well to have children with such plump faces.

Meanwhile . . .

The Homestead Act

On May 20, 1862, when Solomon Butcher was a six-year-old boy still living in the East, the United States government passed the Homestead Act. It said that any man or woman who was at least twenty-one years old, a citizen of the United States, and the head of a family could get 160 acres of federal land free. All the settler had to do was build a simple shack, make some improvements on the land within six months, and live there for the next five years. There was a fee of $18, $14 of which was paid on applying.

When the five years were up, homesteaders paid the remaining $4 and were asked to prove they had lived there with the testimony of two witnesses. This was called "proving up." Then the land was finally theirs.

The problem with the Homestead Act was that it was too easy. Like Solomon Butcher, many of the settlers weren't always capable farmers or knowledgeable settlers. Many didn't even own the proper equipment. All they were really required to do was to build the simplest of shelters, which could have been nothing more than a wagon cover over a hole in the ground, and stay for five years. Many ambitious, hopeful people didn't realize how difficult it would be. As a result, after the settling boom of the 1880s, many pieces of Nebraska land that had been proved up were abandoned.

The Soddy

All pioneers to new lands build houses from available materials to shelter themselves and their families, so when the farmers came to Nebraska they were faced with a very special problem. There were no strong trees for logs to build a log cabin, and no stones to build a European-type house. There were only clusters of brush and willowy trees along the rivers, and plenty of grass.

It's not known where the idea for sod houses originally came from. Maybe it was from the Omaha Indians, who built earth houses, or perhaps it was from the English settlers who had built turf houses for

These are the Chrisman sisters, who each had a claim and took turns living with each other. They are from left to right, including horses:
Bet, Hattie, Lizzie, Lutie, Ruth, and Jessie. Ruth hated this picture. "I look like a horse thief," she said.

temporary shelter in Great Britain. It is certain though that during this period in Nebraska the sod house became the ideal dwelling and its construction was perfected to an art.

First the farmers would select an acre of prairie where the prairie grass was toughest and thickest. This was usually slough grass, blue stem, or buffalo grass. And then they would plow the land with a horse or oxen and a grasshopper plow that cut the grass but didn't turn it over. It was said that "As the cutting plow sliced through the virgin sod, the tearing grass roots made a sound like the opening of a gigantic zipper."

The farmers plowed strips that were about one and a half feet wide and an inch or two thick. They then cut those strips into three-foot-long bricks, and carried them by wagon to the site that had been selected for the house. If there were hills on their homestead, they might build the soddy into the side of a hill, or in a depression. It had to be safe from tornadoes, high winds, arrows, bullets, and prairie fires. Most often the farmers built their houses to face south.

Then, using the sod bricks just like clay bricks, they piled them up into walls, building frames for windows and doors as they went. Cracks were filled with dirt or clay. When they got to the roof, they built rafter poles from what little lumber was available and covered them with a layer of brush or coarse hay and then a thinner layer of sod.

Most soddies were rectangular, typically sixteen by twenty feet or twelve by fourteen feet, with one room—although there have been some that were T- or L-shaped that provided quiet corners out of the wind that to this day is nearly always blowing in Nebraska. The inner walls were smoothed and sometimes plastered. These unique houses were cool in the summer and warm in the winter. When it rained, the roofs leaked terribly. The cooks had to keep lids on their pots while cooking to keep the mud out. Snakes and small animals built their homes in the walls. But when the sun shone, flowers bloomed on the roof.

Soddies were occasionally abandoned when discouraged people went back home.

45

The Beginnings of Photography

Leonardo da Vinci drew pictures of a peculiar invention called the "camera obscura," the "dark room." It was a large box that a man would stand inside. Through a tiny pinhole in one wall an upside-down image of the scene outside the room would appear on the opposite wall. An artist could then slip a piece of paper under the image and trace it. This was the first camera.

Gradual changes occurred to this invention. The room grew smaller until it was just two feet square, lenses were used, and then people began experimenting with light-sensitive chemicals, salts, substances, and surfaces to capture a permanent image. Finally a Frenchman named Daguerre combined a small camera obscura with some light-sensitive materials and took the first sharp, clear, permanent photograph.

He announced that he had perfected this technique of fixing an image onto a silver plate in 1837. The French government bought his invention, and the details became available to the public. News of this wonderful invention reached America in the spring of 1839. Within days and weeks, many Americans had tried their hands and had met with success. The only problem was it took between five and forty minutes to snap the picture.

By 1841 better lenses and methods finally got the process down to less than a minute. Sometimes black or dark-brown metal plates called tintypes were used. These were sturdy, but only one photograph could

A double picture for a hand-held stereoscope.

be gotten this way. Glass was more popular. It was fragile, but many prints could be made from one glass plate.

By the mid 1850s stereoscopic pictures were popular. A picture of the same view was taken from two spots, two inches apart as human eyes are. Then the developed pictures were mounted on cards and viewed through a hand-held viewer called a stereoscope or stereopticon. Because of the two different views, the pictures appeared to be three-dimensional. These were the home videos of the day!

Early Black Pioneers in Nebraska

The first black person to set foot on Nebraska soil was a man named York. He didn't stay long because he was passing through as part of a cross-continental trek called the Lewis and Clark Expedition (1804–1806). York was the personal slave of William Clark, and one of the brave men who actually completed the twenty-eight-month mission covering more than eight thousand miles across the new continent.

When Nebraska was still a territory, slavery was allowed, although it was not common. In fact in 1854 there were only four slaves listed in the

Territorial census, and they were all in Richardson County. The records of Otoe County show there was a man who owned five slaves in 1855, and a year later only four.

I can imagine wandering across the prairie and being startled by the sudden blare and melody of Armsted's brass horn.

During the Civil War Nebraska became one of the routes of the Underground Railroad, which smuggled slaves from the South to freedom in the North. Slaves would escape from Kansas and Missouri through Nebraska City, where they were taken by ferry in false-bottomed wagons across the Missouri River to Iowa and freedom.

But we can see from Butcher's pictures that some black people stayed in Nebraska and made it their home. Many were escaped slaves. Some had served in the Civil War and afterward came to claim their homesteads just as the white people did.

The particular family in Custer County that Butcher photographed in this collection was the Shores family. There were two brothers named Shores and Spees. (They had different names because they had been named for their masters.) The two brothers escaped to Canada by the Underground Railroad during the war, and after staying there for twenty years returned to the United States in the 1880s and, using the Homestead Act, settled near each other. Solomon Butcher made a note that "they have become famous, the young folks as musicians."

What memories these brothers and their families must have had.

I wonder what experience turned this mother's hair so white.

Beginning Again

Times were especially bad in Nebraska in the 1890s. There was a severe drought and a depression across the whole country. There was no rain. There was no money.

Driven from his farm by the drought and forced to support his family, Solomon Butcher had to abandon his history project for a while in 1892 and try to find work. He was elected justice of the peace by his fellow settlers and for three years he worked to help the farmers. It wasn't until 1897, when things began to get a little better, that he returned once again to his photographic history, taking pictures and recording stories.

Then after two years of working diligently on his project once again, Solomon was lying in bed one morning in his own soddy, listening to the sounds around him—his wife cooking breakfast and his children doing the chores. It was March 12, 1899. Suddenly he noticed that up in the ceiling where the stove pipe met the thatch roof, there were burning embers. His roof was on fire!

He shouted to Lynn to bring a ladder, an axe, and water. Solomon became so hysterical that he climbed the ladder in a panic, lost his balance, and fell, knocking himself out cold. Smoke, flames, and heat engulfed the little soddy. His family managed to save only one basket of clothing. His equipment, his photographs, and all the pioneer narratives were lost. Only his glass-plate negatives were safe, because they had been stored nearby in a granary.

Solomon Butcher was forced to begin all over again, almost from the start. He rewrote what he could recall of the text, made new prints from the negatives, and continued his research during the next two years. But by now no one believed in him anymore. He was known as a lazy, crank dreamer who lay in bed while his family worked, and who didn't have the sense to put out a simple fire. "Some called me a fool, others a crank," Solomon Butcher later said of those days, "but I was too much interested in my work to pay any attention to such people."

He had lost all credibility, and his work probably would have been lost and forgotten on that Nebraska prairie, except for a man he'd met, photographed, and included in his collected accounts. Ephram Swain Finch at last came forward. He understood the significance of the history book and shared Solomon's enthusiasm. It was Uncle Swain who gave Solomon the money to finish what needed to be done on the book, which was more photographs and more essays.

Then finally in 1901 the book was finished and published. It was called *Pioneer History of Custer County, Nebraska* and it contained four hundred pages of incredible photographs and wonderful true stories. The first printing of one thousand copies was entirely sold out by Christmas. Butcher's dream, the result of fifteen long years of travel, developing, interviewing, and stops and starts, was finally and deservedly a true book.

Here are some more of the stories and photographs that were finally included in this book of pioneer recollections as told to Solomon Butcher.

Some card-playin', whiskey-drinkin', corpse-hidin' cowboys.

Further Accounts

Corpse in the Soddy

Soddies were very crowded little houses without much room to move around in or add things to. One day an old ranch hand died and all the cowboys decided to congregate and stay together in a nearby soddy to wait for a minister and have a proper funeral.

The soddy was one small room, with a stove, some pots and kettles, a box that doubled as a dining or card-playing table, and a bit of sleeping room on the floor. A half a dozen cowboys would be staying there, plus the dead one. When they were tired of playing cards and finally had to sleep, they stood the corpse up in a corner to make room. Its presence gave them some trouble sleeping, so they opened the door over the corpse to hide it from view.

The next morning when the other cowboys came for the service, and they saw the cards on the table and a jug of whiskey, but no corpse, they were furious and thought it was a hoax to get everyone together.

One of the cowboys had been suspicious all along. "I knew this was a trick," he said. "I would have bet any one of you ten dollars that he wasn't dead." At that, an Irish cowboy named Reddy closed the door and made ten dollars on the spot.

Cowboy Boat Builder

Solomon Butcher came across many interesting characters in his journeys. One in particular was a man named Nelson Campbell Dunlap who was a slim cowboy nearly six and half feet tall. He was well respected and went on to become the manager of the Watsons' ranch in Kearney from 1890 to 1910. The story goes that one day while roping a boar that had gotten out of hand, N. C. Dunlap injured his back and could no longer ride. There is a letter in the archives in Lincoln from his daughter telling how her father had retired from ranching and moved his wife and family back to his original home in Ithaca, New York, where he opened an antique business. His daughter remembers being puzzled when her mother—who had hated Nebraska and its hard living conditions—had cried her heart out when she had to leave it and go back East.

Solomon Butcher took an interesting photograph of this man. It seems

Dunlap must have dreamed of waves and wind and luffing sails as he carved pieces of this boat upon his horse.

I can imagine these girls refusing to open the door to any stranger.

that during N. C. Dunlap's younger cattle-drive days, when he ran cattle from Texas, he spent many long hours in the saddle with nothing to do but watch over the herds. It was during this time that he began to build a model ship and carve the parts while he sat astride his horse. Solomon Butcher captured this man and the finished ship in the eye of his camera.

Home Alone on the Prairie

Jess Gandy had this memory of coming with Charles Penn to Custer County on a hunt in 1876. It was dark, and they arrived at Mr. Murphy's lit soddy on Clear Creek. When they drew near, some dogs began barking and the lights suddenly went out. This was unusual. They knocked on the door.

Finally a little voice yelled: "Who are you and what do you want?"

"We're hunters, and wish to stay the night."

"That's too thin," the voice yelled. "Leave or I will shoot through the door."

"Say, Sis, where's your pa?"

"That's no concern of yours. Leave or I'll shoot."

It turned out that the two little Murphy girls, aged ten and fourteen, were inside, and they were sure the men were either Indians or horse thieves. They held the fort until their parents returned from gathering cedar logs. And then Jess Gandy and Charles Penn joined the Murphys for dinner and the night.

The Good Bad Man

Butcher included quite a few accounts about outlaws in his book. He talked about "the wilds of northern Nebraska where bad men roamed at will, knowing no law but the six-shooter and the Bowie knife." But he was also quite understanding of some outlaws and made excuses for them. He felt they were victims of circumstances and not really "bad men" at all.

One such outlaw was a man who Butcher claimed had been the most depraved outlaw on the plains, a man who had reformed and eventually became an officer of the law. This was a man Butcher referred to as Dick Milton. (Solomon Butcher did not use his real name, in order to protect the man's anonymity.) Milton's outlaw career began, according to Butcher's pioneer history book, through a terrible stroke of luck. Up until that time he'd had a responsible job herding mules and oxen for a freighting outfit. He was a brave man, hard-working and strong.

But one night in a dance hall in Sidney, Nebraska, with the music going, the soldiers and cowboys dancing, and the gamblers and desperadoes drinking and singing at the bar, a pretty girl who was dancing with a sergeant flirted with Dick Milton. An eyewitness told Solomon Butcher that her hotheaded dance partner forced a fight that would end his own career and send Dick Milton into hiding for a long time. There was a terrible uproar, and the two men dove into a fierce struggle. Everyone was trying to get out of the saloon. There were screams, fights. The other soldiers jumped to the sergeant's aid and began to beat up Dick Milton. But then there was a shot. The sergeant fell limp in his companions' arms. The lights went out and now the dance hall fell into total pandemonium.

Somehow Dick Milton escaped into the darkness. A bounty was put on his head for killing a U.S. soldier and he could never stay in one place for very long. He was running from the law, and record has it that he gathered a band of seedy characters around him and did a wholesale business of stealing pony herds from Indians and terrorizing helpless citizens. His adventures included wild Indian raids, diving off cliffs into flooded rivers, close calls with the law and bounty hunters. He had quite a few brushes with ordinary people, and the tales were told again and again.

Cowboy Mischief

One story that was told to Solomon Butcher about Dick Milton obviously made an impression on him. It inspired him to stage the event and photograph it a number of times.

It seems Dick Milton was at a cattle ranch one day and he noticed a cluster of laughing cowboys by the barn. He drew closer to see what was going on, and as he watched he tensed with rage. A cowboy was making an old man dance by shooting at his feet. Every time the old man would stop and beg to sit down, the young cowboy would shoot at his feet again. It was clear that the old man was exhausted and frightened.

Dick Milton looked on for a few minutes and decided to join in. He drew his gun and told the old man to step aside, and then he asked the cowboy to show what skill *he* had as a dancer. The cowboy laughed, thinking it was a joke, and then with a loud ringing shot, the dirt at his feet was plowed up. He began to dance. None of the cowboys were laughing anymore. But this one danced and danced until he dropped in a heap from exhaustion.

Only then did Dick Milton put his gun away. He warned the young man to pick on someone his own size next time.

The Young Kid
Against the Outlaw

The outlaw was not always the victor though. Early homesteaders loved a tale that would put a common man up against an outlaw and show him winning.

"Hold it right there, cowboy. Let's see you dance!"

The story goes that this Dick Milton was riding along the Niobrara River one day, and he must have been lonely and needing a little company, because when he saw another horseman riding ahead of him, he spurred his horse to come up alongside.

The stranger was an awkward young country boy, about eighteen years old with a big revolver stuck in the belt of his patched pants and boots on his feet with bright-red tops.

"Hello, young man. Where you bound?" asked Dick Milton.

"Well, I'm bound west just now."

"I'm going the same way. I'll accompany you. Are you a stranger in these parts?"

"Yes, sir. I've been to see my brother up in Holt County, and they say there's a damned old horse thief named Dick Milton who is scaring everybody out of their wits. I sure wish I could get a look at him. He wouldn't scare me."

Milton must have smiled a little to himself. They rode along, and Milton tried to talk of other things, but the young fellow insisted on talking about the horse thief and how he wasn't afraid.

Finally Milton couldn't stand it another minute and he drew his revolver out. "Young man, you're talking to Dick Milton." He reached over and took the young man's revolver. "You are entirely too careless for this country," he

I can tell how spunky prairie kids were by looking at these two.

said, "and I'll have to ask you to turn your horse over to me and hoof it if you are going any farther."

The boy was pretty cool. "Well, you have the drop on me," he said. "You are perfectly welcome to my horse, but it's pretty tough on a fellow to be turned loose afoot ten miles from nowhere."

"Never mind," Milton said. "It'll teach you a lesson not to be so brazen the next time you meet a stranger. So get off that horse and take to your hoofs."

Incredibly the boy paid no attention, but continued to argue until Dick Milton finally agreed that he could ride until they came to a sheep camp a few miles ahead, and there he would turn over his horse.

They rode along, silently now, and every once in a while the boy would furiously scratch at his leg. "These fleas are eating me up!" he said. "Must've got them at the ranch where I stayed last night."

Milton paid no attention to the boy's complaining and couldn't wait to get to the sheep camp. But when they drew near it, Milton was startled to find himself looking down the barrel of an ugly-looking revolver the boy had fished out of his boot during his frantic "flea itchings."

"Now, sir, *you* turn over them shootin' irons and *you* hoof it."

Dick Milton, seeing the boy had the upper hand, surrendered the guns as graciously as possible and got off his horse. He watched as the boy turned backward on his horse and rode off. The boy never took his eye off Milton as he led Milton's horse away and covered Milton with his own Winchester. When he reached a small hill, he turned and disppeared. Everyone loved this kind of outlaw story.

Years later when Dick Milton finally surrendered, he was tried, spent three and a half years in prison, and came out saying he was tired of his life of crime and wanted to be law-abiding.

This is what Butcher wrote in his pioneer history book: "Dick Milton is at this time a business man in a neighboring state, is marshal for the town in which he lives, and is doing all he can do to atone for his exploits...."

And that was the end of the stories about Dick Milton.

Down a Well

One of the true hazards of prairie life—and Solomon Butcher heard numerous accounts of this—was the homesteader's well. People frequently fell in. Some of these accidents led to deaths of both children and adults, and some falls led to accounts of great endurance and faith. Solomon Butcher included this extraordinary story in his accounts of early days in Nebraska.

F. W. Carlin was traveling in a wagon north of Broken Bow on August

I imagine this father down that abandoned well, and his family wondering where he's gone.

14, 1895. He had taken a wrong turn, and in the approaching darkness he was trying to find the road home. When his horses stumbled, he got off his wagon to check them. Suddenly, without warning, he was falling down faster and faster, like a shot into the darkness. He held his arms straight up, keeping his feet together, and prayed, feeling like he would never hit bottom.

But he did. He was plunged over his head into muddy water. F. W. Carlin struggled and scrambled until he got a foothold and was able to stand. The cold water was up to his arms. The walls of the abandoned well were slimy and lined with a curbing of wood. There was nothing for him to hold on to, but he managed to break off a piece of wood at the bottom, and finding a crack in the wall, he jammed it in and perched there all night.

He looked up into the starry nighttime sky. He could see the top of the well over a hundred feet away—he later learned it was exactly a hundred and forty-three feet—and he could hear his team running away. Without them to mark the spot where he had disappeared, it seemed he would never be found and rescued. There he sat all night, dripping wet and plastered with mud. He didn't know it yet, but he'd sprained his ankle and broken a rib. Everything hurt.

That morning when it grew light, he was able to see the inside of the well and the curbing that had been built to support it. He felt in his pocket, happy to find his knife had not slipped out in the fall. Then with his knife, slowly and deliberately, he began cutting footholds in the wall of the well. It was very slow, but he never lost an inch that he had gained.

He would cut seats for himself out of the curbing wood and sit on them while he worked. Using only one foot because his other foot hurt him so badly, he continued on until he came to a part of the wooden curbing that was tightly fitted and smoothly plastered. There was not a single crack for his fingers to hold on to.

He felt he could go no further, and his only hope was that someone would find him. He sat on his seat and waited. He was shivering with cold and slept off and on through the second night.

Carlin spent the next day sitting on his painful perch shouting for help. He wasn't hungry or thirsty, but he began to give up hope. He thought of his wife and his small son who were waiting for him, a little boy who would never again run to meet his papa. That very thought was too great to bear! What had seemed impossible moments before was no longer impossible. He sharpened his knife on some sand, and in the tight hard curbing he began making more footholds. Higher and higher he climbed, caked with mud, wracked with pain.

After a day he was close to the top. And there to his horror he discovered the curbing was a perfectly smooth four-foot ring, and not only that, it was loose. Water had washed the dirt away from behind it until it was held in place by a single peg. If he tried to put his weight on it, it would probably fall out of place and go crashing down into the depths of the well. F. W. Carlin saw that he had only one chance. He would have to dig in and crawl up between the curb and the dirt wall of the well. And that's what he did.

He eventually reached the top and sprawled on the ground exhausted. He recalled praying on his knees to thank God for sparing him and then he began crawling. He crawled to a road hoping someone would pass, but even by sundown no one had. The next day he crawled again, looking for a house. There was nothing but prairie. He spent another night without food or water.

The next morning he tried again and came upon the soddy of Charles Francis, who took care of him. It turned out that his team had been found the day after he fell in the well, but they had been turned out to pasture and no one had thought to look for the owner!

F. W. Carlin warned Solomon Butcher and his fellow pioneers to watch out for old wells, and to always trust in "a Higher Power."

It's not mentioned in Solomon Butcher's book, but we can well imagine the glad welcome F. W. Carlin received from his wife and son.

Solomon Butcher...

with his mother and his son, Lynn, and his grandson Melvin Lynn.

Solomon Butcher
Never Stopped Scheming

So at last, with the publication of his book, Solomon Butcher had achieved success. His dream was published. The book sold and was very popular, but it seems his success only made him more restless and searching. Now he wanted to compile more pioneer histories of other counties, and maybe of Wyoming, Utah, and Colorado. His wanderlust brought him back to the rut roads, and to support himself further, he began a postcard industry, creating more than two and a half million postcards in his travels that Lynn would develop back at the studio.

When Solomon Butcher was sixty, he was still full of ideas and schemes. He sold irrigated land in Texas, gave stereopticon lectures, did another traveling salesman stint for a grain and flour mill, invented an electromagnetic oil detector that didn't work, made plans for a photographic expedition to Central America that never happened, and even patented an outrageous medicine using some of his medical knowledge that he called "Butcher's Wonder of the Age," which would "drive pain and disease from the human body, giving ginger and pep to the ailing one, having complete control over all stomach and bowel troubles, healing piles, no difference how long standing, as if by magic."

Solomon Butcher probably never knew the power of his own photographic talent and magic. But we know it today as we look back over his photographs—with magnifying glass in hand: clear and crisp pictures of families, and children who have grown up, grown old, and died. Haunting faces, quirky almost-smiles, two-headed dogs who moved when the shutter snapped, skinny horses, sandy bare feet, stiff bonnets, and floppy hats. And all this before the motionless backdrop of Nebraska—its soft rolling hills, its dry sandy soil, and its timelessness.

Solomon Butcher died March 18, 1927. And like him, all the original Nebraska pioneers have come and gone. Cities have sprung up and towns have been abandoned. Nebraska has updated and modernized, but much of the landscape remains unchanged. If Solomon Butcher were to take to his wagon, load up his photographic apparatus today, and head out over the dusty rut roads—but for a jet plane high overhead—he would know exactly where he was. He would still recognize his country.

Nebraska as Solomon Butcher saw it.

And today, a century later, a photo taken by me.

If the woman with the child in her lap is the mother, who is the woman on the right?

Final Word

Sometimes in history there are questions that can never be answered. Answers that are lost with the passage of time. As I look at these old pictures, I have so many questions. Who is the beautiful woman with that family? Is she a teacher? A sister? Where did that boy get his drum? What is that locket on that child's neck? Who is that peeking from behind the door? Did the mother mind cooking for all those farmhands who hung back in the shadows? And what about that black-and-white dog that's in so many of the pictures? Is that a particular breed of mutt that flourished in Custer County at the end of the century? Or is it Solomon Butcher's own dog who followed along in the wagon and managed to get into as many poses as he could?

There will probably never be answers.

When I was in Lincoln, I had the opportunity to have lunch with John

The boy held the drumsticks still in that position so the picture wouldn't blur, yet a hundred years later I can hear the rat-tat-tat.

Carter, the director of the historical archives and an expert on Solomon Butcher, pioneer life, and the history and philosophy of photography, and I asked him, "Tell me, John, if you could step into one of those photographs—go back in time and actually be there—what is it you would ask? What's the one question you'd want the answer to that doesn't come by simply poring over these thousands of photographs?"

His answer was immediate. At first I laughed, but then later looking again at the photos, I wondered, too.

"Where are the outhouses?" he asked.

Acknowledgments

I am very grateful to John Carter at the Nebraska State Historical Society for his help in unearthing, handling, and selecting the photographs, as well as answering my many questions. Any students of history who wish to see more of these photographs can obtain the complete Butcher collection in microfiche from Mr. Carter at the Nebraska State Historical Society through their school or public library.

The map in this book is from the Nebraska State Historical Society in Lincoln. The photographs are all from the Solomon D. Butcher Collection, which is also at the State Historical Society in Lincoln.

The quote on page 44 "The Soddy," is from *Sod Walls: The Story of the Nebraska Sod House* by Roger L. Welsh. Broken Bow, Nebraska: Purcells, Inc., 1968.

Bibliography

Alberts, Frances Jacobs, ed. *Sod House Memories*, vols. I, II, III. Hastings, Nebraska: Sod House Society, 1972.

Barns, Cass G. *The Sod House*. Lincoln: University of Nebraska Press, 1970.

Butcher, Solomon D. *Pioneer History of Custer County, Nebraska*. Denver: Sage Books, n.d.

Carter, John E. *Solomon Butcher: Photographing the American Dream*. Lincoln: University of Nebraska Press, 1985.

Dick Everett. *The Sod House Frontier, 1854–1890*. Lincoln: University of Nebraska Press, 1937.

Lamar, Howard R., ed. *The Reader's Encyclopedia of the American West*. New York: Harper & Row, 1977.

Swedlund, Charles. *Photography*. New York: Holt, Rinehart & Winston, 1981.

Trachtenberg, Alan. *Reading American Photographs, Images as History: Matthew Brady to Walker Evans*. New York: Hill & Wang, 1989.

Welsh, Roger L. *Sod Walls: The Story of the Nebraska Sod House*. Broken Bow, Nebraska: Purcells, Inc., 1968.